TABLE OF CONTENTS

For Audio follow-along, visit www.petekruse.com!
Or search for "2 and 3 chord ukulele songs" on your favorite streaming site!

IT'S A GOOD IDEA TO LEARN THE C AND F CHORDS FIRST.

There are many songs that can be played with just these two chords!

FIRST, LET'S LEARN THE C CHORD.
IT'S PLAYED WITH JUST YOUR RING FINGER.

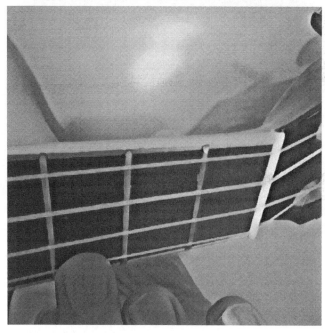

NEXT, LET'S LEARN THE F CHORD.

It's played with your pointer finger and your middle finger.

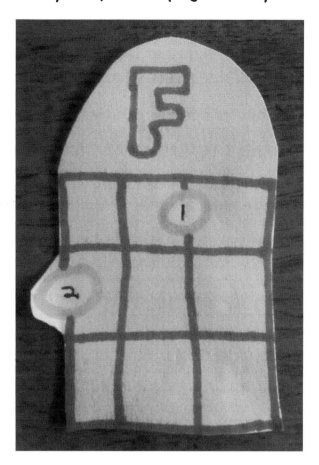

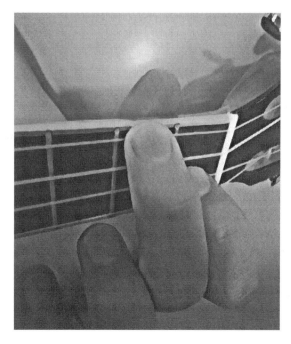

THE NEXT 13 SONGS USE ONLY THE C AND F CHORDS!
We'll learn the G7 chord later - along with songs that use three chords.

1) Are You Sleeping?

```
|  C           |           |           |           |
    Are You sleeping?  Are You Sleeping?  Brother John...   Brother John...
|  C           |           |           |           |
    Morning bells are ringing! Morning bells are ringing! Ding Ding Dong! Ding Ding Dong!
```

2) Mary Had a Little Lamb

```
| F           | C     F     |
Mary had a little lamb, little lamb, little lamb
| F           | C           F     |
Mary had a little lamb and it's fleece was as white as snow
| F           | C     F     |
Everywhere that Mary went, Mary went, Mary went
| F           | C           F     |
Everywhere that Mary went, the lamb was sure to go
```

3) Row Your Boat

```
| F              |              |              |
Row, row, row your boat, gently down the stream
| F              | C      F |
merrily, merrily, merrily, merrily... life is but a dream.
```

4) London Bridge

```
| F                        | C        F    |
London Bridge is falling down, falling down, falling down
| F                | C    F    |
London Bridge is falling down, my fair lady


| F                        | C        F    |
Build it up with wood and clay, wood and clay, wood and clay,
| F                | C    F    |
Build it up with wood and clay,  My fair lady.


| F                        | C    F    |
Wood and clay will wash away, wash away, wash away.
| F                | C    F    |
Wood and clay will wash away, my fair lady


| F                | C        F    |
London Bridge is falling down, falling down, falling down
| F                | C    F    |
London Bridge is falling down, my fair lady
```

5) Itsy Bitsy Spider

```
| F              | C         F |
```
The itsy bitsy spider went up the water spout
```
| F             | C          F    |
```
Down came the rain and it washed the spider out
```
| F            | C        F   |
```
Out came the sunshine and it dried up all the rain
```
|    F         | C       F   |
```
But the itsy bitsy spider went up the spout again

6) He's Got the Whole World in His Hands

```
|        F        |                    |
He's got the whole world in His hands
|        C        |                    |
He's got the whole world in His hands
|        F        |                    |
He's got the whole world in His hands
|        C        |        F        |
He's got the whole world in His hands
```

```
|        F        |                    |
He's got the itty bitty baby in His hands
|        C        |                    |
He's got the itty bitty baby in His hands
|        F        |                    |
He's got the itty bitty baby in His hands
|        C        |        F        |
He's got the whole world in His hands
```

```
|        F        |                    |
He's got a-you and me brother in His hands
|        C        |                    |
He's got a-you and me brother in His hands
|        F        |                    |
He's got a-you and me brother in His hands
|        C        |        F        |
He's got the whole world in His hands
```

```
|        F        |                    |
He's got a-you and me sister in His hands
|        C        |                    |
He's got a-you and me sister in His hands
|        F        |                    |
He's got a-you and me sister in His hands
|        C        |        F        |
He's got the whole world in His hands
```

7) Clementine

```
|      F     |            |
Oh my darling, oh my darling,
|     F    |     C     |
oh my darling Clementine
|     C     |     F     |
You are lost and gone forever,
|      C    |     F     |
dreadful sorry, Clementine.
```

```
|      F     |            |
In a cavern, in a canyon,
|    F    |    C    |
excavating for a  mine;
|     C     |     F     |
dwelt a miner, forty-niner,
|     C    |     F     |
and his daughter Clementine.
```

```
|      F     |            |
Oh my darling, oh my darling,
|     F    |     C     |
oh my darling Clementine
|     C     |     F     |
You are lost and gone forever,
|      C    |     F     |
dreadful sorry, Clementine.
```

```
|      F     |            |
Light she was, and like a fairy,
|      F    |      C      |
And her shoes were number nine,
|     C     |     F     |
Herring boxes without topses,
|     C    |     F     |
Sandals were for Clementine.
```

```
|      F     |            |
Oh my darling, oh my darling,
|     F    |    C    |
oh my darling Clementine
|      C    |     F     |
You are lost and gone forever,
|      C    |     F     |
dreadful sorry, Clementine.
```

8) Michael Finnegan

```
|    F         |              |
There was an old man named Michael Finnegan
|    C         |              |
     He had whiskers on his chin-ne-gan
|    F         |              |
The wind blew them off and blew them on again
| C    |    F    |
Poor old Michael Finnegan, Begin Again


|    F         |              |
There was an old man named Michael Finnegan
|    C         |              |
     Heard this song and began to sing again
|    F         |              |
     Hurt my ears so don't begin again
| C    |    F    |
And that's the end of Michael Finnegan!
```

9) The More We Get Together

```
|    F    |              |
The more we get together,
|  C   |    F    |
Together, together,
|    F    |              |
The more we get together,
     |  C   |    F    |
The happier we'll be.


|   C      |      F      |
For your friends are my friends,
|   C      |    F    |
And my friends are your friends.
|    F    |              |
The more we get together,
     |  C   |    F    |
The happier we'll be.
```

10) Ten Little Indians

```
|   F           |           |
    One little, two little, three little Indians
|   C           |           |
Four little, five little, six little Indians
|   F           |           |
Seven little, eight little, nine little Indians
|   C       |   F           |
Ten little Indian boys.


|   F           |           |
Ten little, nine little, eight little Indians
|   C           |           |
Seven little, six little, five little Indians
|   F           |           |
Four little, three little, two little Indians
|   C       |   F           |
One little Indian boy.
```

11) Go Tell Aunt Rhody

| F | |
Go tell Aunt Rhody,
| C | F |
Go tell Aunt Rhody,
| F | |
Go tell Aunt Rhody
| C | F |
The old gray goose is dead.

| F | |
The one she's been saving,
| C | F |
The one she's been saving,
| F | |
The one she's been saving
| C | F |
To make a feather bed.

| F | |
The goslings are mourning,
| C | F |
The goslings are mourning,
| F | |
The goslings are mourning,
| C | F |
Because their mother's dead.

| F | |
The old gander's weeping,
| C | F |
The old gander's weeping,
| F | |
The old gander's weeping,
| C | F |
Because his wife is dead.

| F | |
She died in the mill pond,
| C | F |
She died in the mill pond,
| F | |
She died in the mill pond
| C | F |
From standing on her head.

| F | |
Go tell Aunt Rhody,
| C | F |
Go tell Aunt Rhody,
| F | |
Go tell Aunt Rhody
| C | F |
The old gray goose is dead.

12) Pop Goes the Weasel

```
| F        | C    F  |
All around the mulberry bush,
|    F     |  C  F  |
The monkey chased the weasel.
|   F     |   C  F  |
The monkey thought twas all in fun.
| C       |  F      |
 Pop! Goes the weasel.
```

13) O Christmas Tree

```
     F                  F
O Christmas Tree, O  Christmas tree,
      C                 F
How lovely are your branches!
      F                 F
O Christmas Tree, O  Christmas tree,
       C                F
How lovely are your branches!


     F                  F
O Christmas Tree, O  Christmas tree,
       C                F
You are the tree most loved!
   F                    F
O Christmas Tree, O Christmas tree,
    C                   F
You are the tree most loved!


    F                  F
O Christmas Tree, O Christmas tree,
      C                 F
Your beauty green will teach me
     F                 F
O Christmas Tree, O Christmas tree,
         C               F
Your beauty green will teach me
```

NOW, LET'S LEARN THE G7 CHORD!
It's played with three fingers.

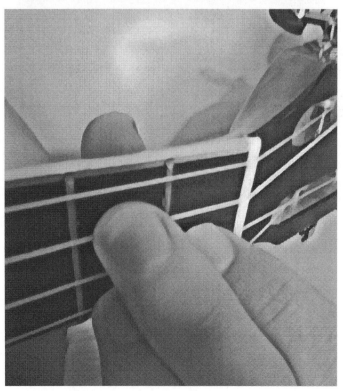

14) Take Me Out to the Ball Game

```
| C        |      G7      |
Take me out to the Ball Game
| C        |      G7      |
Take me out to the crowd
| F        |             |
Buy me some peanuts and cracker jacks
| F      | G7      |
I don't care if I ever get back
|        C      |      G7      |
Cause it's "Root, Root Root" for the Home team
| C     |     F      |
If they don't win it's a shame
|      C      |           |      F  G7 | C  |
And it's "One! Two! Three strikes you're out!" at the old ball game!
```

15) Happy Birthday

```
| C       |      G7      |
Happy Birthday to you
|    G7      |   C      |
Happy Birthday to you
|    C   |     F      |
Happy birthday to you
|    C   |  G7   C   |
Happy birthday to you
```

16) Twinkle Twinkle

```
| C          | F    C |
Twinkle, twinkle little star.
| F     C  | G7    C   |
How I wonder what you are.
| C    F  | C     G7   |
Up above the world so high,
| C    F  | C    G7 |
Like a diamond in the sky.
| C          | F   C |
Twinkle, twinkle little star.
| F     C  | G7     C    |
How I wonder what you are.
```

```
| C          | F    C |
When I go to sleep at night
| F     C  | G7     C    |
Please keep me within your sight
| C    F  | C      G7  |
Please keep watch upon the earth
| C    F  | C     G7 |
Keep it safe till morning light
| C          | F   C |
Twinkle Twinkle Little Star
| F     C  | G7     C    |
How I wonder what you are
```

17) Yankee Doodle

```
| C          | C     G7 | C       | C    G7     |
Yankee Doodle went to town     riding on a pony
| C          | F        | G7     | C         |
Stuck a feather in his hat and called it Macaroni
```

18) Michael Row the Boat Ashore

```
                        I 2
| C        | F   C | C | F  | C   |
Michael row the boat ashore, Halle  lu    jah
| C        |          | (I 2) | C G7 | C    |
Michael row the boat ashore,    Halle  lu   jah


                        I 2
| C        | F   C | C | F  | C   |
Sister help to trim the sails, Halle   lu    jah
| C        |          | (I 2) | C G7 | C    |
Sister help to trim the sails, Halle    lu     jah


                        I 2
| C        | F   C | C | F  | C   |
Jordan's river is chilly and cold, Hallelu    jah
| C        |          | (I 2) | C G7 | C    |
Chills the body but warms the soul, Halle  lu    jah


                        I 2
| C        | F   C | C | F  | C   |
Michael's boat is a musical boat, Hallelu    jah
| C        |          | (I 2) | C G7 | C    |
Michael's boat is a musical boat, halle   lu      jah


                        I 2
| C        | F   C | C | F  | C   |
Michael row the boat ashore, Halle   lu    jah
| C        |          | (I 2) | C G7 | C    |
Michael row the boat ashore,    Halle  lu    jah
```

19) Oh Susanna

```
|   C      |         |         |   G7    |
```
Oh I come from Alabama with a banjo on my knee,
```
|   C      |         |  C   G7 |  C   |
```
I'm going to Louisiana, my true love for to   see
```
|   C      |         |         |   G7    |
```
It rained all night the day I left, the weather it was dry
```
|   C      |         |  C   G7 |  C   |
```
The sun so hot I froze to death; Susanna, don't you cry.

```
|F    |     |  C   |      G7    |
```
Oh, Susanna,   don't you cry for me
```
|   C    |      |     C  G7 |  C    |
```
For I come from Alabama with a banjo on my knee

```
|   C      |         |         |     G7    |
```
I had a dream the other night when everything was still,
```
|   C    |     |  C  G7  |  C   |
```
I thought I saw Susanna coming up the hill,
```
|   C      |         |         |      G7    |
```
The buckwheat cake was in her mouth, the tear was in her eye,
```
   |   C    |         |  C   G7 |  C   |
```
I said I'm coming home from Dixieland, Susanna don't you cry.

```
|F    |    |  C   |      G7    |
```
Oh, Susanna,   don't you cry for me
```
|   C    |      |     C  G7 |  C   |
```
For I come from Alabama with a banjo on my knee

20) When the Saints Go Marching In

```
|           C        |              |          |
Oh when the saints go marching in
|                    |      G7      |          |
Oh when the saints go marching in
|        C       |      F       |          |
Oh how I want to be in that number
        |   C       G7   |   C      |
When the saints go marching in
```

21) Kumbaya

```
        C              F    C
Kumbaya my Lord, Kumbaya
          C                  G7
Kumbaya my Lord, Kumbaya
          C              F    C
Kumbaya my Lord, Kumbaya
F    C      G7   C
Oh Lord,      Kumbaya
```

```
            C          F    C
Someone's praying Lord, Kumbaya
            C                  G7
Someone's praying Lord, Kumbaya
            C          F    C
Someone's praying Lord, Kumbaya
F    C      G7   C
Oh Lord,      Kumbaya
```

```
          C          F    C
Someone's crying Lord, Kumbaya
          C                  G7
Someone's crying Lord, Kumbaya
            C    F   C
Someone's crying Lord, Kumbaya
F    C      G7   C
Oh Lord,      Kumbaya
```

```
          C          F    C
Someone's singing Lord, Kumbaya
          C                  G7
Someone's singing Lord, Kumbaya
            C          F    C
Someone's singing Lord, Kumbaya
F    C      G7   C
Oh Lord,      Kumbaya
```

22) Rockin Robin

C
He rocks in the tree-tops all day long,
C
hoppin' and a boppin' and a-singin' his song.
C
All the little birds on Jaybird Street,
C
love to hear the robin goin' tweet, tweet, tweet.

      F
Rockin' Robin..(tweet, tweet, tweet.)
      C
rockin' Robin..(tweet, tweedely-dee.)
       G7   F   C   G7
Well, go rockin' Robin cause you're really gonna rock, tonight.

23) Working on the Railroad

```
C                              F              C
I've been workin' on the railroad all the live long day
C                                         G7
I've been workin' on the railroad, just to pass the time away
C                              F                   C
Can't you hear the whistle blowin'?  Rise up so early in the morn
C                        G7              C
Can't you hear the captain shoutin'? "Dinah blow your horn!"


C                   F
Dinah won't you blow, Dinah won't you blow
G7                      C
Dinah won't you blow your horn
C              F
Dinah won't you blow, Dinah won't you blow
G7                          C
Dinah won't you blow your horn
```

```
C
Someone's in the kitchen with Dinah
C                             G7
Someone's in the kitchen I know
C                                   F
Someone's in the kitchen with Dinah
 G7               C
Strummin' on the old banjo

                 C
A-playin' fee fi fiddle-y-i-o
C              G7
Fee fi fiddle-y-i-o-o-o-o
C     F
Fee fi fiddle-y-i-o
   G7              C
Strummin' on the old banjo
```

24) Jimmy Crack Corn

```
C                       G7
Jimmy crack corn and I don't care,
G7                      C
Jimmy crack corn and I don't care,
C                       F
Jimmy crack corn and I don't care,
     G7            C
My master's gone away.
```

25) B-I-N-G-O

```
|   C     |  F   C   |
There was a farmer had a dog,
|   C     |   C      |
And Bingo was his name-o.
| C | F   |
   B-I-N-G-O
| G7 | C  |
   B-I-N-G-O
| C |  F  |
   B-I-N-G-O
|   G7    |  C   |
And Bingo was his name-o.
```

26) Swing Low Sweet Chariot

```
        C          F    C
Swing low, sweet chariot,
  C                          G7
Comin' for to carry me home.
        C          F    C
Swing low, sweet chariot,
  C          G7        C
Comin' for to carry me home.


        C                    F        C
I looked over Jordan, and what did I see,
  C                          G7
Comin' for to carry me home.
      C        F          C
A band of angels comin' after me,
  C          G7        C
Comin' for to carry me home.
```

```
        C          F    C
If you get there before I do,
  C                          G7
Comin' for to carry me home.
            C                    F          C
Just tell my friends that I'm a comin' too.
  C          G7        C
Comin' for to carry me home.


        C          F    C
If I get there before you do
  C                          G7
Comin' for to carry me home.
  C                    F        C
I'll cut a hole and I'll pull you through
  C          G7        C
Comin' for to carry me home.
```

27) Amazing Grace

```
    C              F        C
Amazing Grace, how sweet the sound,
      C                   G7
That saved a wretch like me.
   C              F        C
I once was lost but now am found,
      C       G7    C
Was blind, but now I see.


C                        F      C
T'was Grace that taught my heart to fear.
      C                 G7
And Grace, my fears relieved.
        C              F      C
How precious did that Grace appear
      C     G7       C
The hour I first believed.


        C               F       C
When we've been here ten thousand years
        C         G7
Bright shining as the sun.
        C            F         C
We've no less days to sing God's praise
        C        G7     C
Than when we've first begun.
```

28) Jingle Bells

```
C
Jingle bells, jingle bells, jingle all the way
F            C           G7            G7
Oh what fun it is to ride in a one horse open sleigh, Hey!
C
Jingle bells, jingle bells, jingle all the way
F            C           G7            C
Oh what fun it is to ride in a one horse open sleigh


C                                        F
Dashing through the snow, in a one horse open sleigh
                G7                C
Over the fields we go, Laughing all the way
C                          F
Bells on bobtails ring, making spirits bright
                G7                        C
what fun it is to laugh and sing a sleighing song tonight
```

29) Silent Night

```
C
Silent night! Holy night!
G7          C
All is calm, all is bright
F          C
Round yon Virgin Mother and Child
F          C
Holy Infant so tender and mild
G7          C
Sleep in heavenly peace,
C     G7     C
sleep in heavenly peace.


C
Silent night! Holy night!
G7                    C
Shepherds quake at the sight,
F                C
Radiant beams from Thy holy face,
F                C
with the dawn of Redeeming grace,
G7          C
Sleep in heavenly peace,
C     G7     C
sleep in heavenly peace.
```

30) "Go Tell it on the Mountain"

```
F                          C              F
Go tell it on the mountain, over the hills and everywhere;
F                          C              F
Go tell it on the mountain that Jesus Christ is born.


             F                          C              F
While shepherds kept their watching o'er silent flocks by night,
   F                          G7         C         C
Behold throughout the heavens there shone a Holy Light.


F                          C              F
Go tell it on the mountain, over the hills and everywhere;
F                          C              F
Go tell it on the mountain that Jesus Christ is born.


             F                          C              F
The shepherds feared and trembled when lo! Above the earth,
      F                 G7           C           C
Rang out the angel chorus that hailed our Saviour's birth.


F                          C              F
Go tell it on the mountain, over the hills and everywhere;
F                          C              F
Go tell it on the mountain that Jesus Christ is born.
```

Made in the USA
Monee, IL
05 August 2020

37555267R00020